Fire Belly Toads as Pets

A Complete Fire Belly Toads Care Guide

Fire Belly Toad general information, where to buy, care tips, temperament, cost, health, handling, diet, and much more included!

By: Lolly Brown

Foreword

So you've been looking for another hobby, and perhaps you've been mulling over the idea of being a herp keeper - of toads, specifically. Well then, you'd be glad to know that the fire-bellied toad is a good start to your new herp hobby, what if you're one of those seasoned herp keeper who would like to downsize a collection and heard of the ease of caring for a fire-bellied toad? Whichever situation you find yourself, you have come to the right place because this book is specifically written to enlighten you about the husbandry, health, health problems, breeding season, mating rituals, habitat, diet in nature, and in captivity of the fire-bellied toad, and then some.

Understand that the fire belly toads' health in captivity hinges not only on the specific temperature and lighting conditions it needs but also includes the quality of food given to it by a responsible and committed keeper.

Come on a journey which endeavors to draw back the curtains on one of the most popular, highly researched and widely kept-as-pet amphibian around as we reveal details important for a potential keeper should know about the fire-bellied toad, steps to take, what it would take for you to successfully do so.

Table of Contents

Introduction

Sighted in different habitats that are typically found close to water sources, is where the fire-bellied toad, which are in fact a frog, prefers to live. Providing the perfect home for the fire-bellied toad are marshlands, temperate rainforests, swamps, woodlands, forests and sometimes even farmlands.

It is pretty comfortable around water since the fire-bellied toad spends a good portion of its time where bodies of water like small freshwater mountain streams to big slow-moving rivers and lakes.

Fire-bellied toad has eight species and all eight types of frogs occur naturally in those near-water locations ranging throughout Europe and Asia. Most of the eight species of the *Bombina Orientalis* came from China.

Notwithstanding the slight variations of the species, all fire-bellied toads pretty much have the same appearance. All eight toad sorts bear the similar bumpy epidermis, toes which are webbed, and eyes which rest on top of their noggins.

Chapter One: Biological Information

Unlike other toads which are able to extend their tongues at length to capture prey, the fire belly toad needs to get closer to its prey in order to feed, often pouncing on its hapless dinner. And because of its small size, and with the order of the food chain hierarchy, the fire belly toad is also a prey to many larger, stronger carnivores. Not totally helpless in the face of danger, our resilient buddy here has the ability to defend itself by putting up a "fight."

The fire belly toad does so by excreting toxin out of its skin surface which gives off an offending odor and taste to the would-be toad-diner. And that is how our clever little hopper makes a larger, salivating animal want to get back and away from our toad buddy.

Studying up on information about any endeavor an individual seriously wants to get into is a sign of a responsible and committed person. Due to the fact that pets of all sorts and kinds, whether of terra or aquatic origins, have been part of human life and households, humans has had a front row seat and privilege to actually observe and learn about animals in captivity. This being said, we've also made a lot of hits and misses at the expense of creatures of the wild.

Thankfully we now have better access to up-to-date information and continued knowledge with these kinds of animals, and what it would take to be a humane, responsible, effective and successful animal keeper. Read on!

Scientific Name

The *Bombina Orientalis* better known as the Fire-Belly Toad is a name derived from the toad's skin characteristics of starkly colored red-and-black or yellow-and-black pattern markings on the toads' ventral regions, which serve as aposematic coloration. This serves as (an initial) visible warning signal to would-be predators of the toads' alleged foul taste. The other areas of the fire belly toads' skin can either be green or dark brown.

In the event of a confrontation with a potential predator, these toads would commonly react with an Unkenreflex ("Unken" is the German word for fire belly) - a reflex defense mechanism to stave off and dissuade would-be predators from making a meal out of it. When the Unkenreflex is carried out, the fire belly toad would arch its back, raise itself on its front and back legs allowing it to display only the aposematic coloration of its ventral side.

Types of Fire Belly Toads, Origin, and Distribution

Of the 8 frog species of the *Bombinatoridae* family, the *Bombina Orientalis*, or the Fire Belly Toad is endemic to in China and Russia. The other frogs of the *Bombinatoridae* family are comprised of the following:

Bombina bombina

The *Bombina bombina* or widely known as the European fire-bellied toad is native to mainland Europe. This specie is listed as least in danger on the IUCN list of endangered species, along with supporting evidence of why it is not deemed endangered.

Bombina lichuanensis

Also known as the Lichuan bell toad is endemic in Hubei and Sichuan in China. This sort of fire belly toad is on the red list of being vulnerable of becoming endangered due to habitat loss according to the records of the IUCN.

Bombina fortinuptialis

Also known as the Large-spined Bell Toad or Guangxi Fire Belly Toad and hails from Guanxi in China and like its previously mentioned cousin from a neighboring Chinese province, this frog is also on the IUCN red list whose population is threatened by habitat loss.

Bombina microdeladigitora

Otherwise known as Hubei Fire Belly Toad, is a specie whose name is considered a synonym of Bombina maxima (Bombina maxima, commonly known as the Yunnan firebelly toad), come from the regions of Yunnan, Guangxi, Sichuan, Hubei and Guizhou in China and in the Northern regions of Vietnam nearest to China.

Bombina orientalis

Better known as the Oriental fire-bellied toad is actually a frog species found in Northeastern China, adjacent areas of Russia and Korea and are listed as of least concern in terms of endangerment with the IUCN.

Bombina pachypus

The Apennine yellow-bellied toad is a higher class of frog from the Bombina family tree and is on the red list of endangered species of the IUCN. Threats to its population include pollution, forced change of habitats due to draining of swamps, and diseases.

Bombina variegata

The yellow-bellied toad lives in mountainous regions and hilly countries in the middle and southern areas of Europe. It is largely spread out across the high hilly areas of middle and southern Germany and can also be spotted in a few places on the Upper Rhine River Plains.

Size and Physical Appearance

Most of these species are typically 1.6 to 3 inches in length. Epidermis color, of the spectrum of eight species, depends on the sort of toad in focus. The variation of these frogs skin colors range from yellow to brown, orange, green and white.

Our frog on spotlight, the Fire Belly Toad, has vividly colored red-and-black or yellow-and-black pattern markings on its ventral regions, which serve as aposematic coloration, warning and repelling potential predator attacks. As with all the frog sorts of the *Bombinatoridae* family, our very own fire belly toad has the same bumpy skin, webbed toes, and big, bug-eyes situated on top of their heads.

Whereas the common *Bombina Orientalis* is usually tinted a grass-green and black on the upper, visible portion of its body, other individuals of the frogs could vary in dorsal color from a drab brown to bronze. Fortunately, even the most unattractive *Bombina Orientalis* has a vibrant red-orange underbelly whilst other fire belly toads can be of red, orange or yellow in color.

Growth Rate

The fire belly toad completes its transformation between two to two and a half months. Tiny fire belly toad tadpoles hatch in 3-4 days and remain motionless and attached to the stems of plants or leaves, where the female lays the eggs, for 2 days. Sustenance is gained as the tadpoles absorb the yolk sacs.

When the larvae reaches a full body length between 3.8 to 4.8 centimeters when transformation from tadpole to juvenile toad begins. Success depends on the genetic factors, its nutritional status, and temperature of the fire belly toads' enclosure. If all these requirements are conducive, transition from tadpole to juvenile should commence.

Developing tadpoles start to show interest as they gravitate toward shallow areas of water or look for flat surfaces which give a way to get to resting areas above the surface of the water. A notable increase is detected in swiftly changing tadpoles as the individuals seek and survey moist land by still using their tails which are almost at full length.

It is usually on day 10 when the hind legs of the tadpoles emerge. Front legs appear between days 19 - 22. It is now important that the vivarium housing the tadpoles is well laden with aquatic plants in order for the little froglets to reach the water surface with ease. Making use of floating cork bark a gravel islet or a fashioned platform, the tadpoles will exit the water.

Some tadpoles begin exploration as they climb up small plants when the tail length becomes by 10 - 20 % and as they begin to chase after bugs. Metamorphs or newly-emerged fire belly toad froglets will not eat for about 3-4 days after exiting the water. During this time there are pretty dramatic changes happening to the fire belly toad involving physiology, morphology and behavior. Feeding is interrupted at this time because the intestines and mouth of tadpoles metamorphosing are reconstructing.

As soon as they show arms and legs, the juvenile will begin to work for a brief period of combined tail and limb use shortly followed by a total shift from tail to leg thrust. The juvy-fire belly toad uses these limbs to walk, jump and swim. The head shape of the fire belly toad changes along with the function and shape of its eyes, mouth and intestines

After the 3 - 4 days of the metamorphosis process is up, the keeper will need to provide the froglets with fruit flies in large amounts as nutrition is critical to their survival during this delicate period of physical change. Experienced keepers also feed the froglets 10-day old crickets, aphids caught in the wild, tiny leaf invertebrates, and springtails.

A juvenile fire belly toad will have a body length, from the tip of its snout to its cloaca, of about 12 to 18 mm. The total length of the adult fire belly toad ranges from 3.8 to a little over 5cm. A fire belly toad reaches sexual maturity between 1-3 years of age and has a total body length of about 4 cm.

Longevity/Lifespan

Many factors are taken into account when discussions of the fire belly toad's longevity come up. Depending on the conditions of their environment, whether captive or otherwise, the little toads do and will have to contend with a number of things.

The survival of the fire belly toad, whether in its natural habitat or in the captive care of its keeper hinges on a number of things. Fire belly toads in the wild have been observed to be able to live up to about 5-7 years in its natural habitat. As rules of nature dominate their instincts, toads go where the food can be found, having said that, the same rule applies for the fire belly toad's predators. Sickness and disease, aside from animals which prey upon our usually colorful friends here, are likely possibilities of length of lifespan success.

A real grave threat to this species is the prevalence caused by humans is habitat loss due to territorial occupation. The diligent maintenance and the keen observation of a keeper, once under the keepers care, is primarily what allows the fire belly toad and its cousins to thrive well in captivity. These resilient little guys have been reported to enjoy lengthy lives of up to 12 - 15 years under the watchful eye and care of a meticulous keeper guardian.

Chapter Two: Fire Belly Toads as Pets

Keepers of these tiny leapers find utter enjoyment as they observe their pets antics and development with quiet amusement. We say pets in the plural because it has come to many fire belly toad keepers attention that having more than one of these little guys makes the frogs seem happier when in groups, although a lone fire belly toad survives and thrives well on its own. It will be up to the keeper to decide on whether to start with a bunch of these generally colorful frogs or if the keeper guardian chooses to maintain just one.

Your decision about the number of fire belly toads to keep should become more apparent and concrete as you read on and find out more about their care and husbandry needs. Now as much as a fire belly toad usually live a solitary existence in the wild, keepers of this amphibian sort have found and observed that fire belly toads have no real big issues sharing space with a few more of its same-sort kin as long as provisions for their needs are met and conditions in their captive habitat are conducive to the lot.

Discover the joys of maintaining a group of fire belly toads in a fully functional, fully furnished and tempered vivarium, and understand why countless other amphibian keepers are held in fascination by these amicable, friendly toads.

What Makes It a Great Pet

Many reptile and amphibian keeper's, most notably those who have scaled down their collection and/or passed up the chance at the onset of their hobby to care for the fire belly toad, have rediscovered the pleasures of their herp hobby when they tried their hand on maintaining a bunch of fire belly toads.

Housing fire belly toads in a fully decked out vivarium, one which is well lit and plant laden allows the keeper to observe their very own bunch of leapers at their best and find them a real pleasure and utterly enjoyable to watch.

For starters, unlike most amphibians, fire-bellied toads are surprisingly more active during the day. It is their diurnal tendencies of the fire belly toad which allow keepers to easily observe their pet's behavior. You, as the keeper guardian of a group of these friendly hoppers will be able to witness their individual and group habits which will almost certainly include aggressive strongholds exerted by males whilst they grip onto almost anything that moves in their general area, as their companions call out squeaks of distress calls as they splash around in their fashioned pond in what would look like a group hug. These joys too can be experienced by you, our novice keeper and you shouldn't pass up the chance to do so if given the opportunity.

Legal Requirements

Founded to ensure the protection of the general world population and resources of flora and fauna CITES, also known as The Convention on International Trade in Endangered Species of Wild Fauna and Flora is an agreement amongst international world governments which helps makes sure that the business of exchange of plants and wild animals internationally is monitored, documented, and regulated. These rules were compiled and imposed to ensure the survival of all plants and animal species endangered by irresponsible and opportunistic groups and individuals out to line their own pockets for personal gain without regard about keeping balance.

Whilst under initial formation back in the 60's, ideas then were vague and relatively new. However with the progression of time, the urgency for more stringent laws and bylaws became more urgently apparent and could no longer be ignored. This was largely due to the alarming rate of illegal trade of flora and fauna which had become bolder and more blatant. It was during this time, reflecting more than ever, that the dire need to set more stringent laws and regulations to curb, stave off and halt the indiscriminate practices of some that made such a huge, damaging impact on the rest of the balance.

Billions of dollars is the estimated amount of the annual trade of animals and plants throughout the world, wherein live plants and animals of a very diverse selection are taken from their natural habitat, captured, killed and used for a number of products and purposes from making timber, tourist souvenirs, pharmaceutical and holistic medicines, musical instruments, exotic leather goods, and food products, just to mention a few.

The exploitation and illegal trade level was staggering and the urgency could no longer be ignored lest nature suffer irreparable damage. The loss of habitat, even to this day with development disturbing animal and plant species in their natural environments, is a reality many have no clue about and the thoughtless randomness of infrastructural development has made it harder for these once peaceful collective of the planet's residents to cope up with due to the actions of humans, resulting in many of these plant and animals lives to come close to extinction.

Fortunately, concerned governing bodies such as CITES and IUCN, sustainability of these trades, puts into good practice and use that is geared toward the betterment of humankind - hoping to not be such as heavy of an impact toward the contribution of the natural and animal kingdoms - makes it possible to ensure sustainability of these life forms for the continued balance of the existence of animals, flora and humans alike.

Tee method of making a declaration and have a country be tied up with the regulations stipulated by CITES is called, 'accession, 'approval', ratification' and/or 'acceptance', and are all equivalent to legal procedures, actions and penalties. These laws and regulations, however does not bind all countries of the planet but only those States who have signed the Convention when it open and available for signature back in March of '73 to December of '74 are included in the regulations. The fire belly toad we are talking about in this book, is thankfully one of the more popular and easier to repopulate in captivity, hence it is classified as one of the least endangered of its sort.

There are animal species and plant specimens which show up on the endangered are list but fall under the clause of special circumstances for trade, which is medical research and could have a higher likelihood to gain approval for trade given that an authorization grant for importation and exportation has been provided with a permit to do so. Still, a number of general prohibitions and special exceptions need to be followed and considered even after obtaining a nod from all governing, involved and concerned bodies.

The fire belly toad or the *Bombina Orientalis* is not in any way shape or form on any of CITES lists of endangered species with special restrictions, but it is still up the potential keeper to keep it this way by ensuring a humane process of acquisition through responsible research and in depth analysis of what is best for all before closing any deals of sale and taking home any of these quirky toads.

Myths or Facts?

It is no myth at all that the skin of the fire belly toad is indeed toxic if one is to come into contact with its bumpy surface. The good news is that it is not deadly to humans and the most damage it can cause is an adverse skin reaction which can be avoided with proper fire belly toad handling knowledge. You will read up more about how to handle one later on, should a situation deem it necessary for you to handle it at all.

Pros and Cons of Owning One

Amphibians and reptiles in captivity had very slim chances of survival in the past living with humans because of our lack of know-how and understanding to how they lived and thrived. Because of the advances of herp medicine and the urgency of needing more herp experts to cater to the growing number of herps kept as pets, our scaled friends and as well as amphibious buddies stand a better chance of survival under our care.

Still, it is not as easy to find a herp vet as we would think but there are specialists of reptile and amphibian animal care who keeper guardians can call upon now more than ever. It is really important for the potential keeper to get one on their speed dial even before the actual acquisition. It is best to get in touch with your local herp society to get as much networking done, not only to answer and calm the potential keepers doubts and misgivings, but also to get assurance that there are other hobbyists who've been where you are now and

Ask yourself if you are ready to be the keeper guardian the fire belly toad deserves. And answer this question with all honesty according to what you know in your heart you are capable of and what would prevent you from giving your potential fire belly toad the care it would need.. The potential keeper is to have a good head on their shoulders and a realistic view of what is expected of them to be able to care for these amusing little fellas.

Chapter Three: Purchasing and Selecting a Healthy Breed

Randomly pointing out one of our little buddies to take home is a definite no-no. This wouldn't be how, you, our potential herp keeper, would want to start out your hobby responsibly. The success of raising a group of these green hoppers hinges largely on the commitment and awareness of the undertakings entailing the tasks of which a dedicated keeper must be enlightened. And along with many factors and details a keeper needs to understand is the vitality of recognizing a healthy fire belly toad as well as where to look and who to deal with before actual acquisition.

Responsibility does not end upon purchase. It is just the beginning. It is wise for you, our promising keeper to arm yourself with all the pertinent knowledge about our green buddy thus enabling you to care for them with great confidence. Read on to determine how you can learn to spot and recognize what you should be looking out for when you start checking out places on where to get your very own gang of amiable fire belly toads.

The next sections aims to reveal to you, our budding herp enthusiast, of what you will need to be mindful of when choosing the individual to deal with, a sound place of acquisition, what to ask, what to expect and what behaviors, traits, physical conditions, clues on present frog health - visible or otherwise - and indications that will speak of the frogs' future wellness under your care.

Remember that knowing what to look out for is just part of the whole parcel. Your continued commitment and diligence after purchase will play a very large role in the fire belly toads

Where to Buy a Fire Belly Toad

There will be a few options for you to check out in your quest of looking for the fire belly toad group you will want to take home. Knowing what to ask, determining that transaction will be on the up and up and being able to spot what would indicate the wellbeing of the lot of your choice are some of the things you want to learn early on as these will assist you in making a sound decision on the people you will want to deal with later.

Keep in mind that your best bet would be to get in touch with your local herp society to ask around about fire belly toad owners who have gained some recent success in breeding their lot and who may be also searching for possible keepers interested in taking in one or more of these little aquatic dwellers.

Characteristic of a Healthy Breed

Take stock of your options regarding the business of who to deal with when you have made the decision about the fire belly toad being a constant in your life.

Whereas a pet shop is perhaps a potential keepers easiest bet on finding and acquiring a fire belly toad, it would be strongly recommended by this writer to first consider touching base with your local herp society to make inquiries if there are any known keeper guardians who have had breeding success recently.

Fire belly toads bred directly from the source in captivity is most usually guaranteed to have in better overall condition and better health than that of those caught in the wild. Individuals caught in the wild would've surely suffered some sort of trauma not only due to the stress of being handled roughly at the onset of capture but likewise during transport, eventually to be thoughtlessly stuffed into confining, overcrowded encasements to be shipped off to pet shops all over the globe.

If there are no captive-bred fire belly toads in the area and the pet shop is your only options, then read on to find out what you need to be watchful for and keep an eye out for because you want to have the highest chance of raising one from a pet shop successfully.

You first want to silently observe as you take mental notes. Make an ocular inspection of the enclosure where the toads are kept.

- Is the enclosure clean?

- Spot out any unhealthy or sick looking animals inside the enclosure?

- Are there other species of cohabitating with the toads?

- The fire belly toad shows a measure of elusiveness but will slowly respond positively to the presence of humans in its presence

- It is a healthy eater with a good appetite (try to time your visit when it is feeding time)

- The animal takes to water with ease and gusto

- There is no discoloration nor is there sagging of the fire belly toads skin (an indication of malady)

- The toad is mobile and able to do all the things it is naturally gifted to do without hindrance or difficulties

- Make certain all digits are present and without injuries

- The eyes are to clear, without discharge and must be responsive to movement

- Ears and nostrils as well are to be free of any discharge

- There are to be no signs of gashes, nicks, scars, wounds or sores

- Its mouth is able to open and close and does not gaped open when it is at rest

- The body is free and clear of any signs of skin infections or bacterial fungus

- The fire belly toad is not hostile

Other species of semi aquatic animals are usually mixed in with fire belly toads in pet shops - a dangerous situation which exposes all the animals to exchange of foreign pathogens amongst the species originating from different parts of the world - a breeding ground for sickness and poor health.

The risk of physical trauma is almost a given for any enclosure housing mixed species, from toads making attempts at dining on other animals within their cages. It wouldn't be the first time a toad would try making a meal out of the leg of newt. It is an aggressive predator with an even bigger appetite, so this could equate to injuries during struggle. Should this be the case in any of the pet shops you may visit, then it would be best to look elsewhere.

Characteristics of a Reputable Breeder

Hoping to save you some research time, we have compiled information that is relevant to your desire of being keeper to a fire belly toad or two (or more!). These are collective reports, and stories from seasoned herp enthusiasts and aficionados who have been more than happy to share useful bits and important details on how to avoid the frustration of having the deal with flowery sales talks and empty promises of individuals whose only aim is to line their pockets by making a quick buck off of you.

Decision making will largely fall on the potential keepers' deduction of whether they are dealing with upstanding individuals, but we largely discourage acquisition of any sort of pet which a keeper has no possibility of seeing for themselves before sealing a deal. "Why?" you may ask. You see, with no possibility of seeing the pet with your own eyes, without the advantage of checking out its present conditions, you will not be able to identify tell-tale signs that would indicate the overall wellness and health of the fire belly toad.

Should you feel satisfied by the person online you are dealing with, there is still the matter of how the toads will get to you. Once the lots of toads have left the care of the people you will be dealing with, they will have no control over the method of transport and how long it would take for the animals to get to your doorstep. Another consideration would be the cost of transporting the little guys and of course the assurance that they will be safe throughout the journey of getting to you. These are additional procedures you will have to monitor along with the additional costs of cargo and handling.

We start off with the most obvious choices:

- One place that abounds with possible contacts, the Internet. The Internet is a virtual marketplace where information on breeders and their locations are prevalent. And you will indeed find a lot of these people. There are quite a bit of concerns that arise when choosing this route of purchase, though.

- Another available and very likely place to locate fire belly toads is a pet shop. The issue most pet keepers have with pet shops is that these establishments are usually the "dumping grounds" for illegally caught, shipped and sold pets - whether reptile, mammal, or amphibian.

- o Even with the best of intentions, pet shops are not usually privy to how these animals were captured, shipped or purchased; much less know of the animal's medical background or history - an important bit of information which would spell your success or failure of raising them when you take them home. What is disturbing is how the animals are housed - usually in cramped enclosures and mixed with other species, not taking into regard compatibility or if shipped in the possible foreign pathogen contamination of the animals.

- o This latter bit of housing conditions result in stressed animals, some often falling ill without outward, visible signs (until taken home) and aggressive behavior that could compromise the whole lot of toads.

Some Recommendations

- Check out your local herp society. That would be a sound start to kick off your inquiries.

- Your next best bet is to visit your local amphibian shelters to ask if they happen to be housing a fire belly toad or two.

  - Should this be your choice of acquiring your future amphibians, you will still have to ask relevant questions like how the toads came into their possession, its history, reasons why the previous keepers chose to give the toad or toads up (Did they get in over their heads? Were the toads ill? Was there a display of excessive aggression? Or did they simply move away? Etc.). Other questions you would want answered would be if the former keepers handed the shelter pertinent historical and medical records.

- Your best option, aside from getting in touch with the herp society in your locality is to get in contact with a fire belly toad keeper with recent breeding success or an actual breeder of reptiles and amphibians with an upstanding record of transparency and one who can give you guarantees, ideally in your general area.

There is good news, though. Breeding practices have improved greatly through experience and countless keepers have gained great success in multiplying their collection and would be ready and eager to share best practices with you.

You will find dealing with upstanding breeders a breeze, so don't hold back when you ask questions related to their breeding methods. Thrown in questions about where they are housed, what they are fed, traits, temperament, quirks and moods of the animal. Most importantly inquire of its medical history, possible health conditions and obtain medical records that would show procedures it may have undergone. It shouldn't be a surprise if the breeder offers more information about the amphibians in question as a breeder of good repute will want to be assured as well of the home their temporary wards will be joining.

The advantages of dealing with an upstanding breeder are the assurance of being given firsthand information which works toward your favor. They will also be able to point you to other breeders in the area whom you can network with later. They are not only knowledgeable of the individual animal, they will be just as concerned about how well you will fare raising a toad or two, and will be the best people to give you tested methods and best practices. To top off these countless advantages, they will be in the position to give you guarantees on the animals wellness other places wouldn't be in the position to offer and most importantly, they will most certainly be able to recommend the services of a seasoned herp vet who will be a vital player in the success of you raising your future fire belly toads.

Make it your job at this early stage of your studies about the fire belly toads, their needs, and the tasks you will be responsible for before sealing any deals. To sum up this section of this chapter on Characteristics of a Reputable Breeder, here is a quick look once again:

- You want to be well informed of this undertaking of seeking out the best possible breeders to talk to and with whom you will close a deal. Doing so will allow you to make a responsible and sound decision in your search of your fire belly toad.

- Breeders of upstanding repute will not pussyfoot when supplying answers to any and all of your questions about the fire belly toads in question.

- Responsible and humane breeders of fire belly toads would house the toads using the appropriate housing equipment for their temporary, transient amphibian wards.

- The experienced breeder understands the importance of knowing who to call in case of a sick amphibian. They would have an experienced herp vet on their speed dial.

- The upstanding and well-reputed breeder shall also pose their own set of queries to ask the potential amphibian keeper about the home conditions of the buyer.

- A thoughtful breeder would be concerned about the housing requirements the potential keeper has set up or intends to set up for the amphibians. He/she may also ask the future fire belly toad keeper about the measures they have taken to fit and furnish the enclosure of the toad lot.

- This breeder would be more than willing to graciously impart vital advice and tips to the potential fire belly keeper not only to dispel their doubts on the commitment of the future keeper, but also to gain a measure of assurance that the fire belly toad lot will be paired with a suitable keeper, and to ensure the safety and healthy future of the fire belly toads.

- Breeders who come with a high recommendation rating could possibly be open to parting with some minor supplies and sundries already in use by the fire belly toads which could help enhance and promote a more conducive vivarium atmosphere to make sure that the welcoming comforts of home needed by the fire belly toads are met satisfactorily.

- A responsible breeder would have also begun the primary inoculations needed by the amphibian before handing the toad over to you.

- High standard breeders will have a complete and comprehensive medical file of the fire belly toads' medical history, as well as any procedures and tests the fire belly toads may have previously undergone.

List of Breeders and Rescue Websites

This next section is a possible kick off related to your search for breeders. Let us gently remind you that you should in no way advocate the purchase of any animals, most especially your desired fire belly toad online, sans the opportunity to check out the amphibian and its living conditions for yourself.

Our hopes are that you will be in close proximity of a reputable breeder or at the very least get one to point you in the right direction.

It will be apparent to you as you check out these sites that most breeders would often have supplies needed by a reptile and amphibian keeper to set up a comfortable space or vivarium for your future toad friends, which will be available for purchase - a convenience that will most likely not require your attendance - much like online shopping for a shirt or a pair of shoes. These virtual hobby-supply shops would also be likely to have pet food suppliers in their contact list, making your search for food resources later on a breeze.

This short list of breeders hopes to oil the wheels and get your search started. It is still highly recommended that you go beyond this list of suggested breeders we have come up with and that you make your own calls to get in touch with the breeders of good standing we talked about earlier.

Breeders and Rescue Websites in the U.S. and U.K.

Back Water Reptiles
<http://www.backwaterreptiles.com/toads/fire-bellied-toad-for-sale.html>

Petco
<https://www.petco.com/shop/en/petcostore/product/fire-bellied-toad>

Big Apple Herp
<http://www.bigappleherp.com/Firebelly-Toads-Group-of-3>

Reptmart.com
<http://www.reptmart.com/p-631-firebelly-toad-for-sale.aspx>

Pet Smart
<http://www.petsmart.com/live-pet/live-reptiles/fire-belly-toad-4032724.html>

Josh's Frogs
<https://www.joshsfrogs.com/complete-care-kits/frog-kits/fire-bellied-toad-kits/show/all.html>

LLL Reptile

<https://www.lllreptile.com/articles/144-fire-belly-toads/>

The Reptile Report (Rescue)

<http://thereptilereport.com/fire-bellied-toad-rescue-help/>

Amphibian Rescue

<http://amphibianrescue.org/tag/oriental-fire-bellied-toad/>

Pet Solutions

<https://www.petsolutions.com/C/Live-Frogs/I/Ornate-Horned-Frog.aspx>

888 Reptiles UK

<http://www.888reptiles.co.uk/645.html>

Preloved UK

<http://www.preloved.co.uk/classifieds/pets/reptiles/for-sale/uk/fire+bellied+toads>

Adpost UK

<http://www.adpost.com/uk/pets/9312/>

NewsNow UK

<http://www.newsnow.co.uk/classifieds/pets-animals/toads-for-sale.html>

Chapter Four: Requirements Before Buying a Fire Belly Toad

This next chapter focuses on important facts and vital nuggets of details geared toward the proper husbandry, conducive environment settings, setup of your fire belly toads enclosure along with furnishings, fittings, sundries and quality of environment, including lighting, temperature, substrate and plants.

We mentioned earlier, the great advancements of medical care of amphibians (and reptiles, alike) has allowed these once medically overlooked sort, which historically struggled in captive care to survival, a better fighting chance of living long healthy lives. More importantly, it must be said that most herp experts in the field of reptile and amphibian medicine have determined that almost all if not most illnesses, ailments, diseases, malaise and poor health conditions of an animal is caused by the improper setup of the animal's enclosure as well as shoddy maintenance.

Wrong temperature settings, improper timing of temperature regulation, poor lighting exposure, improper ranges of humidity and especially enclosures which are unkempt and unsanitary are some definitive causes of animal malaise and illnesses of amphibians in captivity. The first thing that a keeper of amphibians should check when their pet gets sick is the enclosure, its conditions and its cleanliness. Sanitation is a great oversight that must be addressed immediately upon detection of an ill amphibian. A sanitary environment will have no place for bacteria, mold, fungi or viruses to thrive.

A responsible keeper should understand and be aware that sanitation is first and foremost in the avoidance of illness being introduced in the animal's enclosure. It is an imperative rule to abide by to allow your amphibian pets the best chances of surviving and thriving well under your mindful care. The next sections are aimed at detailing the how's of setting up a proper vivarium that will be provide a promising enclosure which will promote a healthy environment to allow your soon-to-join-the-ranks fire belly toad. Not only will it be a place which would give your new toad-pets a shelter of good equilibrium but also a space which will provide the right conditions in order for it to maintain good health.

Fire Belly Toads in the Wild vs. in Captivity

In their natural environment out in the wild the fire belly toad has been noted to be able to flourish in nature as it lives, exists and feeds off the bounties of their territorial range with a lifespan of a little over decade - and a few years if it is lucky. The fire belly toad in its natural habitat and territorial location is seen to be an opportunistic eater whose appetite is triggered by movement. The possibilities of the fire belly toad not having enough to eat shouldn't be a problem for them since they chose to be where the conditions are rife for a plethora of food choices available to the toad for its dining pleasure.

Out in the wilderness and in the midst of their natural habitat the fire belly toads are in plain sight and are vulnerably exposed to a variety of different situations which a captive fire belly toad would not have the misfortune of experiencing given that it was bred in captivity.

When in captivity, the burden of food sourcing falls on the frog-keepers shoulders, and it is up to the amphibian keeper to provide the frog with a variety of food choices. Readily available and able to aptly provide the bulk of food of the fire belly toad's diet are crickets. Offer each toad about two to six pieces of crickets a minimum of once a week and a maximum of two times a week.

The possibility of not being able to meet it nutritional requirements is slim to none in an area rich in the fares the fire belly toad favors. The alarming reasons of nutritional lack stem largely from fragmentation or loss of wetlands is due to infrastructural intervention. Once disturbed, these semi-aquatic frogs will have to move away to find better sources of food and habitat, exposing them to the dangers of predators.

Lacking food to eat, vital to its strength and wellbeing, the soundness of its health is greatly compromised. Not getting its required balance of nourishment does not result in immediate starvation but a continued basis of food deficiency will make the fire belly toad vulnerable to a host of maladies, diseases. Fire belly toads not only share territorial hunting grounds with other fire belly toads, but also with other semi-aquatic reptiles and amphibians like lizards, newts and salamanders which favor closely similar dietary choices. In addition to the competition the *Bombina Orientalis* has to contend with for the same types of bugs, it is also in danger of predators which do not lurk too far from their favored digs and which are drawn to the places where the toads are known to inhabit. Having to deal with predators and the stresses of escaping is reason for the tiny amphibian to become anxious and hyper alert.

The list of predators which prey on fire-bellied toads is long from snakes, cats, foxes, lizards, and birds along with a few species of large fish and some water snakes. The egg clusters female fire belly toads lay in the water, as well as tadpole hatchlings unfortunately have their own sort of predators underwater.

Illness and malaise in the wilderness is another challenge fire belly toads will have to experience by themselves without medical attention; a situation that their captive cousins will hopefully not have to endure. Disease and sickness acquired in their natural habitat is a reality of the fire belly toad when in the wild. Out in its natural territory a sick or diseased fire belly toad has no possibility of being given medical attention or treatment. The ailing fire belly toad will just have to put on a brave front and live the remainder of its life suffering from the illness in silence as it tries to get away from the animals which prey upon it.

In comparison, the lifespan length of the fire belly toad, when in captivity, notably increases due to the availability of medical care when attended to by an expert herp vet. The presence of a keeper who is mindful of the minute changes in behavior of a sick captive fire belly toad a higher likelihood of getting the medical care it needs, increasing its chances of survival, as well as living healthy and well. Having keeper guardians attend to providing them sustenance and attending to their daily needs, captive fire belly toads are spared from going through the often harrowing challenges and frequently dangerous settings of their natural habitat in the wild. Fire belly toads in captive care can reportedly live up to 15 years, with some keeper reports of their *B. orientalis* wards enjoying long lives of up to 20 years, given optimum care.

Housing Requirements

Keep in mind that the semi-aquatic nature of fire belly toads tend for them to prefer floating in shallow water with their toes barely in contact with a solid bottom. Setting up an enclosure for a fire belly toad or a group of them will depend on you - your call as keeper allows you to put the enclosure together as simply or as intricate as you wish.

Fire-belly toads will need a fairly big enclosure to thrive well wherein they are able move freely without being confined in cramped spaces, to do what they would normally do in the wild. In fact a 15-gallon standard aquarium will be sufficient room to house up to three adults. If you are looking for a bigger lot of fire belly toads to rise, a group of six or more can be kept together in a 20-gallon tank. Make sure to cover the tank opening with a tight-fitting screen to avoid breakouts.

- Room temperature is ideal for housing fire-belly toads, with an optimal temperature ranging between 65 and 78 degrees Fahrenheit.

- Monitor the water temperature in the tank and keep the temp between 60 - 72 degrees Fahrenheit. Never allow water temperature to exceed 80 degrees Fahrenheit.

- Hot conditions exceeding 82 degrees are dangerous, but cooler temperatures of 50 degrees (and no lower) do not present a problem.

- Make use of a thermometer to monitor the temperature.

Start by treating the water for the tank a day before with aquarium additive to neutralize the chloramines and chlorine. A day after water treatment, fill the 15-gallon tank with an inch or two of the pre-treated tap water.

Get a big slab of cork bark and let it float on the water surface. As an alternative, you may choose several large, smooth rocks like granite, slate or quartz which you will want to arrange to stick out the water to serve as an area of land. The land surface area you fashion out of the rocks should be roughly equal to the surface area of water. Be mindful to regularly change the water in these sorts of simple systems to rid the water of waste like dead feeder insects and feces. You will need to factor this task of treating and changing the aquarium water as regularly as possible, two to three times a week. At this time, no substrate is required.

Submerging a shallow water container into a coconut husk fiber substrate or other soil-like substrate is an alternative method you can opt to for when you set up the aquarium. Choose a water receptacle which is able to cover roughly half the bottom area of the terrarium. You can cover the coconut husk fiber with pieces of cork bark along with artificial plants, which you can position on top of the substrate.

Make sure that the substrate remains moist by adding a little bit of water to the substrate surface once or twice each week, but be mindful that the substrate never becomes soggy r waterlogged. Change the water in the water container daily to maintain sanitation. Normal household humidity levels of 30 percent or more is sufficient as humidity is not as important as temperature. In particularly dry conditions, you may spray the enclosure daily with water to maintain a moist enclosure environment and temporary humidity increases much like to what the fire belly toads would experience in its natural, wild environment after rain.

Given some time, light and sufficient moisture, live Java moss (*Vesicularia dubyanacan*) strategically planted along the fashioned shoreline will flourish and hold gravel in place. Other hardy houseplants which can grow directly in gravel like Pothos (*Epipremnum Aureum*), or Heartleaf Philodendron (*Philodendron hederaceum*) can be planted on the land area for a sturdier land grip.

Parrot Feather (*Myriophyllum Aquaticum*) or a Cryptocorine water plant species will do well in the water. Other good aquatic plant choices for the fire belly terrarium would be Java Fern (*Microsorum pteropus*) and Anubias species attached, tied and fastened onto pieces of submerged rocks or driftwood with fishing line.

Tied and fastened with fishing line onto submerged pieces of driftwood or rocks water plants like the Anubias species and the Java Fern (*Microsorum Pteropus*) also make suitable aquatic-flora choices. So as to make way and space for plants in a semi-aquatic, planted aquarium the water depth can be increased to half a foot or more. Not only will adding live aquatic plants pretty up the fire belly toad enclosure, but the plants, in time, will also work in maintaining up to par water quality, as the plants help produce a stable environment in the enclosure where only partial water replacement may be needed a few times a month.

It is vital to provide sufficient lighting in the enclosure in order for the plants added to the terrarium thrive and flourish. Your fire belly toads are not finicky in this aspect and the toads themselves do not need special lighting of any sort. The aquatic plant however, is a different story. If you do decide to add plants to the terrarium (and it would be quite advisable for you to do so, allowing a better recreation of the fire belly toads natural habitat) you will have to affix a couple or so of standard T8 fluorescent tubes of over the terrarium. Fluorescent light tubes with a natural color temperature range between 5000 and 6500 Kelvin are good choices and look best.

.

Maintenance

If you recall, almost all herp experts have zeroed in and agree that most amphibian and reptile ailments and diseases stem from and are the result of unkempt, unclean, shoddy habitation. Your task as the responsible keeper of these magnificent little frogs is to make sure your amphibian wards are housed in a well maintained vivarium. Make sure that you factor the cleaning and maintenance of the enclosure into your weekly schedule and stick to that schedule until it is becomes a habit.

By scheduling a regular, weekly cleanup of the enclosure you not only ensure a clean vivarium conditioned and primed for healthy living for your fire belly toads, cleaning it out will also make the enclosure a better smelling, better-to-look-at, tidy and efficient toad vivarium pleasing to the eyes. A thorough once-over will suffice for the enclosures weekly maintenance; however, you must make it a point to take more time to do a detailed general cleanup of the terrarium.

Remove all furnishings and fittings including soil and substrate materials, place and organize them in a box then set them aside. Clean out the enclosure completely and diligently; use a scrub to scrub all corners, nooks and crannies with organic solutions diluted in water. Allow the enclosure to completely dry.

Once the enclosure is dry, put in a fresh bed of substrate, replace the all the plants fixtures and furnishings back and make sure that all fixtures that need to be secured are securely fastened. Make sure that there are no loose wires and that all heating and lighting sources are working well.

To clean out the water of a vivarium with aquatic plants set on substrate, you will need to vacuum the substrate to get as much of the dirt, dead leaves, feed remnants and feces lifted from the substrate material. You may remove plants attached to rocks or cork barks by hand, plants permanently planted on the substrate aren't removable pieces, so you will need a filtration system to cycle, clean out and replace the water.

- Heating: 65 and 78 degrees Fahrenheit
- Humidity: 30% level
- Water: 50-72 degrees Fahrenheit

Costs of Housing Requirements

The cost of housing requirements of the fire belly toad is perhaps the easiest terrarium to set up because of the minimal requirement of the fire belly toad for regulated temperature heating. Should you choose to furnish the vivarium with semi-aquatic plants, the plants may need the extra lighting and heat.

Purchasing supplies from a pet shop would be the easiest way to gather all that you would need to set up the terrarium. Buying everything brand new will cost a chunk of cash and having an expert set up the terrarium professionally will add to the cost. It would be a good time to use your imagination and begin networking with other amphibian keepers to get tips and suggestions.

Dollar costs of an all-new, all-shiny set up will depend largely on how imaginative you are. Still, you will be spending much less than most hobbyist whose pets require round the clock temperature regulation, heating pads, basking lights, vents, humidifiers, as well as UVB light fixtures etc. The fire belly toads terrarium will also cost much less in annual maintenance costs in terms of electricity costs.

Costs of a basic Fire Belly Toad enclosure:

- 20 gallon glass terrarium (brand new) will cost about $100 - 150 and could include one 20 Gallon Glass Aquarium, one LED hood, one Tetra Mini UL Heater, one Tetra Whisper 20 Filter, one artificial Boxwood Plant Mat, and artificial plants.
- T8 Fluorescent tube bulbs 5000K (4 pcs) will cost around $44.00
- Dimmer will cost about $ 28 - 38
- Timer is around $13 - 15
- A digital thermometer ranges between $6 - 12
- Back up heaters for cold winters will set you back about $15.00
- A water filtration system (up to 30 gals) would cost anywhere from $26 - 35

Factor in your initial supply of substrate and furnishings such as cork barks, aquatic stones, semi-aquatic plants and a quarantine tank for when you need to separate a fire belly toad from the rest of the population and you would have a rough idea of how much you will be initially spending.

As early as now, begin to imagine how the fire belly terrarium would look. Take to paper and design your vivarium careful not to leave out any of the essentials that will be required by your new group of pet toads.

Flea markets, bargain shops and garage sales are good places to find some if not most of your terrarium needs. Don't forget that the internet is a haven for buyers and sellers of all brand new and secondhand items, which include sundries, fixtures, furnishings and equipment for your terrarium.

Should you opt to purchase items that were pre-used, make certain that each piece and item is sanitized and thoroughly cleaned before placing it inside the terrarium. No one wants to risk a healthy fire belly toad or any pet for that matter, by having it fall ill simply because you were just too lazy to do the necessary work of ensuring all items cleaned and sanitized.

Chapter Five: Nutrition and Feeding

Don't get fooled by our little frog buddy's cuteness factor as a hindrance to it being a fierce predator, because it is and it has quite an appetite for its small size.

Triggering the fire belly toads' instinct to gravitate toward prey is movement of any possible food source which happens to be in its range of lunge. In the wilderness, the Bombina is noted to dine on various aquatic and terrestrial insects which include worms, flies, mites, snails, water beetles, springtails, amphipods, and backswimmers.

When in captivity, the burden of food sourcing falls on the frog-keepers shoulders, and it is up to the amphibian keeper to provide the frog with a variety of food choices. Readily available and able to aptly provide the bulk of food of the fire belly toad's diet are crickets. Offer each toad about two to six pieces of crickets a minimum of once a week and a maximum of two times a week.

Whether in the wild or in captivity, seeing how a fire-bellied toad eat is quite a fascinating sight, the toad's very long and very sticky tongue would shoot out of its mouth to grab and catch hold of an insect and would be pulled into the toad's open mouth.

Favoring small invertebrates, like insects, make these little hoppers carnivores with a diet largely comprised of bugs, with some rare exceptions like spiders, larvae and the occasional worm. But we'll dig deeper into their diets later. The tables are turned when it is prey though. Being the little creature that it is, our little buddy has to defend and protect itself from a number of predators which prey on them in its natural environment.

Find out about the specific diet requirement of your future pet-hopper and learn about additional supplements you can use to increase the intake of its nutrients to the best of the fire belly toads advantage. Keep in mind that the quality of food intake along with vitamins and supplements given to a captive fire belly frog is what will spell the success or failure of your interest and intent to raise one or more of these amusing amphibians. Get a clear view of foods, food portions and feeding frequency of the fire belly toad and give yourself the best advantage to raise your fire belly toad right.

Food in the Wild vs. in Captivity

When in the midst of its natural habitat of the wilderness, the fire belly toad is one cunning sneak of a predator to some of its more favored insect fare of the aquatic or terrestrial sort and these would comprise of amphipods, mites, water beetles, snails, worms, springtails, and backswimmers.

Our frog buddy has quite an appetite and a plethora of bug choices available to it in the wild. The list of potential food sources would also include flightless flies which can be found aplenty in swamplands, marshlands and slow-moving bodies of water. Not spared from the constantly ravenous fire belly toad are minute ghost shrimps, small guppies, shrimp, and hapless, slow moving snails,

Captive fire belly toads have it easy with their keepers being responsible for providing them with food they would otherwise have to hunt for themselves. Choices are perhaps not as vast or as usually fresh as the fire belly toad would prefer but a hungry toad and one bred and raised in captivity would be used to feeding differently than its free-in-the-wild kin. Crickets are the most common of food picks of keepers to feed their pet frog.

Nutritional Needs of Fire Belly Toads

Make it a point to feed your fire belly toad's crickets and mealworms. Toads will thrive on live crickets and mealworms, which you can purchase at a pet shop and should be the main staple of your fire-belly toad's diet. You must feed your toads as many crickets and worms that they can consume in a 15 minute period. Size of crickets should be no bigger than the fire belly toads head to avoid choking.

Additional fare (insects) you can add to your fire belly toad's diet aside from the main staple of live crickets and mealworms that your toads can benefit from are guppies, and snails. These food sources can be added to their water. Being the active animals that they are, they would benefit being offered live food sources in their aquarium.

All food given to the toads should be live. Fire-belly toads are not able to recognize non-living food sources, and non-living foods can quickly contaminate your toad's enclosure.

Make sure to supplement your toad's diet with vitamins and minerals to complement their meals. Adult fire belly toads do benefit from added vitamins and minerals in their diet. There are crickets which sold that are supplemented with vitamins and minerals needed by your toad to get a balanced diet. Toads usually benefit from supplemented crickets every one to two feeding periods.

Discuss offering supplements with your herp vet before introducing any to your fire belly toad's diet. You want to make certain that the supplements you give the toad lot are healthy and safe for them. Many insects have a tough indigestible exoskeleton which can cause your fore belly toad bowel impaction and should not be offered to them. All insects should ideally be gut loaded with a well-balanced serving of vegetables as well as calcium and vitamins before being offered to fire belly toads.

You may also look into offering Insects that are easy to get hold of like superworms, king mealworms (zophobas), earthworms and waxworms. Other insects which you can occasionally offer as variety which can be bought locally or through mail order are butterworms, and silkworms. Make sure that these meals are given live and set on the ground of the terrarium.

Primary Foods

Hungry toads with big appetites are able to stuff their mouths with adult crickets easily. Calculate the length of the cricket to be an approximate measure to the size of its head which would be about half an inch or thereabouts. This would be the ideal sized cricket safest to feed our amiable buddy frog. To ensure nutritional requirements are met lightly roll the crickets and cover it with a high-quality powdered nutritional supplement before placing the frog food into the enclosure.

A few times every month, give your little fire belly toad a treat and mix it up by offering it a serving of earthworms, which you may opt to cut up - no room for the squeamish with this pre-serving task - and put the worms on a shallow dish like a small jar lid and set the dish on the base of its enclosure, making sure that the worm parts are still moving. As long as they are, the frogs will dine on them. Remember that toads don't recognize non-living foods.

Other food varieties which can be offered are soft-bodied insect larvae and wax worms. There are fire belly toads which will feed on black or Tubiflex worms, which can be found in pet stores along the fish department. When you are ready to serve up these food sorts, always remember that they are best set on land (soil, ground) instead of placing the portion in water as it would normally be served for fish in an aquarium.

Other food fare that your fire belly toad would gobble up with hungry gusto are tiny ghost shrimp, snails, small guppies if any of them were chanced upon venturing into shallow areas of water sources in the wild by our dexterous frog friend. Springtails, newly hatched crickets and flightless fruit flies can be fed to juvenile toads.

Tips on How to Feed Fire Belly Toads

- Always offer and feed your fire belly toads live prey as they do not comprehend the idea of dead food.

- Offer food with a pair of tongs or tweezers and avoid using your bare hands lest it mistake one of your digits for food.

- Live prey offerings must be eaten within 24 hours of the buying or they will expire soon after purchase.

- Supplement your fire belly toads meals with gut loaded insects sprinkled with vitamins and minerals

Amount Required for Fire Belly Toads

Fruit flies or pinhead to week-old crickets should be fed to baby fire belly toads and can be their main source of food until they are ready for larger fare.
Small earthworms and waxworms are toad favorites and can be given to adult fire belly toads. Some keepers have experimented and discovered that if given at the early onset of adulthood, some fire belly toads could learn to welcome non-living foods such as strips of raw fish or beef offered with a pair of tweezers.

Mature fire belly toads enjoy a diet of three to four-week-old crickets raised commercially. To measure the correct prey size, take care that the length of the crickets offered is no bigger than the width of the toad's head. Enhance the food of your fire belly toad by supplementing its food with a combination of amphibian vitamin-mineral powder containing calcium at least twice a week. Not doing so can result in the fire belly toad to suffer from calcium deficiency and it could end up with metabolic bone disease.

Let's delve a little more into the required diet of juvenile and adult fire belly toads:

The answer to the discussion with regard to the frequency of feeding your Fire Belly Toad as well the amount of food you offer it will differ with its age. A good rule of thumb is to give and feed it only the amount it will acceptably eat within a span of 15 minutes. Each toad's appetite will be different from each other with one possibly eating more than the others, however, fire belly toads are typically voracious eaters with hearty appetites. Keep a feeding journal and note your observations of what and when the fire belly toad eats. Maintaining a journal will allow you get to know the amount of food your fire belly toad is able to consume at various stages of its growth. As for frequency, fire belly toads like routine, so feed them at the same time each day.

In the wild a fire belly toad is able and will eat up to 1000 bugs each day. Whilst a fire belly toad in captivity has no need to eat as much on a daily basis, toads must be given sufficient rations of food during the summer period - the period of the year when nature instructs their body clocks to eat more in preparation for winter hibernation. During winters, fire belly toads in captivity eat much less, and sometimes not at all. Do not be alarmed (unless you notice other signs that would indicate illness). Gluttons by nature, it could be possible to overfeed a fire belly toad, but never probably never to the point of obesity. Remember that in the wild they are capable of gobbling down 1000 insects a day. A healthy toad is one that has a hearty and voracious appetite and it is quite impossible for a toad to die of obesity. Truth of the matter is, toads are plump, leaning on fat, animals and this physical trait is partly why they are so adorably lovable.

Juvenile toads can be fed small, non-flying fruit flies (Fliegen) and crickets (Grillen) freshly hatched; both of which are readily available and can be purchased at zoo shops.

The juveniles are swift at learning how to hunt for their prey on the water surface, on terrain and on plants. The fire belly toad is able to jump powerfully, far and high, closing distance and direction to its prey in mere seconds and soon after - a matter of hours or a couple of days can attain catching successes close to 90%.

Even in ostensibly insurmountable situations fire belly toads are capable of sorting out approach tactics to successfully catch their food. They have a great, big appetite and must be fed once or twice a day during months that experience higher temperatures.

Juveniles should be offered and given increasingly bigger prey, like worms (Würmer), young crickets (Heimchen, Grillen), hairless insect larvae, house flies (Hausfliegen), and, if and when available, 'meadow plankton'. The more mature, adult fire belly toads have a wider food range and would gobble up practically any captured or given insect which could include butterflies (Schmetterlinge), long-legged spiders (Spinnen), grasshoppers (Heuschrecken), large worms (Würmer), and on occasion and rare happenstance, stray wasps (Wespen) and bees (Bienen).

Ravenous adults capture and may swallow small prey which sizes up to measure a length not much smaller than themselves as well as worms measuring a length of 2 or 3 times their body length. The only foods they prefer are those that move, and are living prey which they like to pounce upon. Its prey and potential fire belly toad belly-buster will meet its end by giving away its presence with an indication of life through a trivial movement or, methodical activity like routine breathing, movements of antenna or limbs. It could merely be resting from flight or have stopped at mid crawl but once the fire belly toad senses a prey, it lunges at it and latches on the the prey til it is no more.

The toads will eat ay flying, creeping or gliding prey, and all kinds of animals that fall on the water surface. Food diversity is fundamental for normal growth development. The food quality of the catch is tested and tasted in the toad's mouth cavity with unpalatable food rejected and forcefully spat out.

Pre-mating toads typically do not separate to feed and the couple may even catch each end of the same worm. Who ultimately wins the squiggly, live fare is not a matter of 'politeness,' but a matter of power. The general rule is: the fire belly toads (and its Bombina kin) go where their food is.

Chapter Six: Handling Your Fire Belly Toad

The fire belly toad is by nature opportunistic in their habits of hunting for, foraging for and eating their meals and is usually spotted in rather shallow stretches of water. The *Bombina Orientalis* species easily colonize, mate and breed in simulated bodies of water like paddy fields and ditches, despite their preference for bigger areas of standing water.

In northern areas of their range, the fire belly toad may hibernate in streams, although they more commonly seek out mounds of leaves or would choose to withdraw beneath tree roots for this purpose, often gathering in groups in convenient localities of this sort.

This section is compiled information on why not to handle, how to handle and when it may be necessary to handle your fire belly toad. It will be the shortest section of the book as you will soon discover why. Read on to discover the toxic appeal of the fire belly toad and how its skin makes it possible for it to stay alive another day in the presence of dangerous predators.

How to Handle Your Pet Properly

The *Bombina Orientalis*, our very own Fire Belly Toad, is much like many if not most frogs and must not come anywhere close to your mouth much less eaten. The skin of these frogs produces foul tasting toxins and could be harmful. Should you make the mistake of touching or rubbing your eyes after handling one of these little guys, you are sure to experience an intense burning sensation.

Now, should this unfortunate scenario happen, make haste and rinse out your eyes with lots and lots of clean, fresh water. Should you have little cuts or nicks on your hand or skin where the frog had rested its body you will feel that same burning sensation seemingly coming from the inside out.

You need to wash your hands and any part of your body the toad had come into contact with immediately. Over time the belly coloration of fire belly toads bred, raised and cared for long term in captivity, usually fades to yellow-orange or yellow-tan instead of the stark, bright red. The pigment cells of the skin responsible for the strikingly bright belly coloration have vesicles to store carotenoids, plant-derived yellow and red pigments which include xanthophylls and carotenes.

The "magic" of the fire belly toad epidermis is that it is able to store pigment. The trick to help promote the development of the stark red coloration is through the crickets you give to the toads. How, you ask? Several hours before giving the crickets to your fire belly toad, feed the cricket color-enhancing fish flakes or some grated carrots.

The alteration in the ventral color of fire-belly toads collected out in the wilderness can be attributed to the availability of xanthophylls in their habitat to a degree. This gives reason as to why some fire belly toads caught in the wild appear to have red bellies and others have orange bellies. Influencing xanthophyll pigments in your fire belly toad's diet will enable to manipulate and experiment with your fire belly toad's skin color.

Chapter Seven: Breeding Requirements

You may eventually want to try your hand at breeding your lot of fire belly toads later given its propensity to provide hours of calming entertainment as you get front row center seat to their daily ins and outs, year after glorious year. Even if you have no initial inclinations to do, you still wouldn't want to be caught unawares of when mating and breeding season begins for the fire belly toads.

Discover the mating behaviors of the fire belly toad, the mating and breeding season, how often this cycle comes around and what to expect after a successful mating. Be prepared to provide the proper environment and equipment to allow an egg laden fire belly toad the best chance of laying her eggs in an adequate environment which will promote a healthy place for her cluster. All these and more are details you should expect to be revealed to you in the next sections you go over.

Breeding Basics

It is around late spring when fire belly toads mate and breed. The female fire belly toad would lay a clump of about 50-300 gooey, sticky eggs called toad-spawn onto the stems of plants or leaves hanging above water. Curiously, it takes fire belly toad tadpoles a couple of years to come into full development and maturity. An adult fire belly toad typically attains an adult length of about 2 ½ to 3 inches long.

Sexing

Male and female fire-bellied toads look like twins to the untrained eye. Even to the trained eye many differences aren't obvious, and the amphibians themselves sometimes mistake male for female. Slight differences in physical characteristics, and behavioral and physical changes come mating season, give insight into what kind of fire-bellied toad you're dealing with.

Note that while females and males will breed, aggression will not typically result from keeping two of the same sex.

- **Tubercles**
  - The male and female fire belly toads are typically covered in tubercles. Tubercles look like bumpy warts on their epidermis. Tending to show more and more-defined tubercles on their backs, whilst females typically appear to have smoother skin. Some males have a lot more and much bigger tubercles than other males which gives them an overall bumpier looking skin, whilst there are some female fire belly toads which have smaller and a lot less tubercles than other female fire belly toads. However it isn't unusual to find smoother skinned males and females with bumpier looking skin.

- **Forearms**
  - You may suppose that your fire belly toad has four legs but in fact its "fore" legs are its forearms. The female forearms are typically more slender in appearance than those of the male fire belly toad. It isn't a very tell-tale sign and you probably won't even notice this until

you a male and female side by side together, but it is a subtle difference that could help you identify the sex of the toad.

- **Nuptial Pads**
  - When the fire belly toads breeding season commences in the early spring of each year the male fire belly toad, as observed and documented by the Smithsonian Institution National Zoological Park, develops nuptial pads on both their first and second fingers. The pad which emerge at this time of the year allows the male fire belly toad to hang on fast to the female fire belly toad when mating season is nigh. On the other hand, nuptial pads elude females and they never go through this mating transformation.

Grasping and Mating Process

If there was ever a question in your mind about the gender of your fire belly toads and you've wondered about which is which and who is what, mating season will certainly provide an answer to your query. Should you be raising two of these toads and one grasps and latches onto the other, you can bank on the grasper to be the male frog as females have no inclination to that behavioral trait. Here's the clincher though - the one grasped isn't necessarily the female fire belly toad. Male fire belly toads would typically grasp and grab other male's toads that would usually protest and make loud fuss and attempt to get away by struggling free. However, females also attempt to free themselves of this grasp-hold by twisting and turning their bodies if they are not willing or ready to copulate.

Another ritual the male fire belly toad carries out during mating season is let out a mating cry, which the University of Michigan likens to a bark. When picked up unexpectedly or when startled, the female would let out a noise as well, but the bark-like mating call is a sound exclusive only to the male fire belly toad.

The commencement of the spawning period is marked by the males, who begin to utter their very distinct calls. One of the main triggers for this ritualistic behavior during late spring seems to be sunlight, therefore if possible, change the location of the fire belly toads' vivarium so as to get it closer to a window, where it can catch the early rays of morning sunshine. Do take care to clinch that it doesn't get left there the entire day though, as the temperature inside the enclosure could quickly spike to a fatal level.

This is the phase at which the male toads so-called 'nuptial pads' will be visibly apparent, displayed as swellings on the inside of its fore feet. During this time of year, when looked at from above, females would seem to appear to be more rotund too, specifically as they begin to swell up with eggs.

These fire belly toad-frogs commonly reach an adult length of approximately 2 inches. Sexing can be a challenge to determine, but if you look hard and if you know what to look for females tend to possess a slightly fuller build, whilst male toads appear more slender. Their skin may also appear smoother, but this is a less reliable indication, in terms of sexing.

Fire belly toads are unusual, because when they mate, they show 'pelvic amplexus', with the male toad grabbing the female from behind her back legs instead of her forelegs, as is more usual in frogs and toads.

Incubation Period

Spawning typically happens during the night and little brownish eggs called clusters, numbering anywhere from 30 to more than 100 are laid in the water, on the surface or stems of aquatic vegetation or other submerged items.

Strips of plastic bags placed in the water have also been used as oviposition sites in captivity. If the eggs are fertile, will notice the ovum splitting and tadpoles developing within a day or two you, at this point, separate the eggs and any items they were laid and transfer these to a separate aquarium. Tadpoles should come out from the egg jelly three to 10 days after being laid. It will take one to five months for the fire belly toad metamorphosis to be complete.

Tadpoles will grow to a little over an inch in length before each develop arms and leave the water. They are not picky eaters and can be raised on aquarium fish flake foods to start them off. When front arms develop, reduce their water depth to an inch or so, and give them access to land. Juvenile toads are not as brightly colored or pretty to look at as adults, being mainly brown in color and about three-quarters of an inch in length at metamorphosis. It takes close to at least one full year for maturity to be attained. .

Many individuals who have bred fire-bellied toads have reported that the bright ventral coloration of captive-bred fire belly toads doesn't display as vividly intense as that of those in the wild. Because of this reason, think about providing the toad a dietary supplement that would provide carotenoids to juvenile toads, and feed the little teardrop-shaped tadpoles a carotenoid-rich fish flake diet. Carotenoids provide amphibians the colors yellow, orange and red, and a captive diet lacking in them may contribute to dull-colored animals.

Fire belly toads are hardy amphibian pets which display a number of attractive traits and qualities, like bright colors, diurnal activity and interesting behaviors. They sure are common, and with good reason. The most vital part of their care is giving them the proper environment. Top that off with varied diet offerings, and you will certainly have made a long-lived group of toads for you to enjoy watching for years.

Hatching

The spawn will be wrapped around aquatic plants, and will need to be transferred to a separate aquatic terrarium for hatching purposes. The water temperature in the hatchling enclosure must be maintained at around 25°C (77°F), providing the enclosure with a heat pad under thermostatic control, instead of using an aquarium heater stat.

Females could lay as many as 250 eggs during the summer season, usually in clusters of up to 45 eggs at once, so be ready for regular spawning during this period.

Reproducing Fire Belly Toads

With super affordable, imported fire-bellied toads prevailing over the amphibian pet trade, there is not much monetary incentive to breed them in captivity. Still, it can give an interesting chance to observe the entire lifecycle of an amphibian. And, if one were to know where to look, they will find that there are fire belly keepers who are in fact breeding for a wee bit of profit and for the pure pleasure of doing so, sharing their successful yield with other interested keepers of these toads. Of the four accessible Bombina species, the *Bombina Orientalis* is the most commonly available and is the easiest to coax into reproducing.

Attempt to raise a bunch consisting of at least several male/female pairs. Raise as many as three extra males, to every single female, as this may also help promote breeding. Male toads can be told apart from females by the appearance of dark nuptial pads, but these are only seasonally visible when the fire belly toads are ready to reproduce. Males also possess more muscular forearms compared to females, but the best way to tell them apart and to differentiate the sexes is to listen. If you see a toad calling out boisterously, there is little doubt it is a male toad, although female toads can give out less-boisterous distress calls. The call of a male is distinctly loud and rhythmic.

In the wild, fire belly toads reproduce after a period of winter hibernation. In captivity changes in seasonal temperature encourages the breeding flurry. If your aim is to breed your fire belly toads, keep them in a room which naturally goes through changes in temperature during varied times of the year, like the basement or an enclosed porch. Keep their environment near 60 degrees or lower for a month or so to hasten the process.

When temperatures begin to warm up, make sure to of more frequent water changes and feed them heavily. Big water changes copy the conditions of spring rains, which is the time wild fire-bellied toads begin to breed in nature. If all goes as planned, female toads shall swell with eggs and pairs will engage in amplexus. Brace yourself as a female fire belly toad can produce new eggs every two to three weeks.

Nesting Requirements

The young tadpoles should start to hatch after around five days, depending on the water temperature, and although at first, they will appear immobile, this is quite normal. They are digesting the remains of their yolk sacs at this stage, before they become free-swimming.

Rearing is generally very straightforward, with flaked fish food being useful for this purpose. Powder it first by rubbing it between your fingers. Choose a flake mix such as Nutrafin Max Color Enhancing Flakes, which contain a natural coloring agent derived from red algae, or Tetra Pro Color Premium Flake. This in turn should help to ensure that young toads display the same intense coloration on their under parts as their parents, once they metamorphose.

Whichever brand you choose, only buy a small tub as you will not need large amounts. In fact, it is vital not to overfeed the tadpoles, causing food to be left uneaten in their quarters. If this happens, the water quality will deteriorate rapidly, endangering their health. Other amphibian-specific foods can be added to their diet as the tadpoles grow larger, such as bloodworm or daphnia from Tetra's Delica range. These can be used straight from the packet and do not need to be refrigerated. Both are supplemented with vitamins and other nutrients too.

Be prepared to separate the tadpoles as they grow into smaller groups of similar size, so as to minimize the risk of any cannibalism. Carry out partial water changes regularly, using a test kit to keep a check on water quality, and ensure the replacement water is at the same temperature as well.

Chapter Eight: Life Stages of Fire Belly Toad

With prime quality, and abundant food, young fire-belly toads will develop quite quickly, and could be mature by the time they reach a year old. There is no immediate need to rush and pair them up though, since they have a surprisingly long lifespan, and can effortlessly exist for 12 years, and some individuals have been known to live into their twenties!

Discover the different stages of development and growth of the fire belly toad and get a heads up on what to expect and what to look out for at this delicate stage of growth and metamorphosis.

Allow us to whet your imagination as we get you excited about the upcoming additions to your home and keep you enthused and excited about the impending arrival of your own groovy bunch of squawkers and barkers who're great opportunistic food pouncers.

Life Stages

By the time the tadpoles reach about six weeks old or so, their hind legs will have started to make an appearance, swiftly followed by their front legs about five days after the latter, making them look more like the frogs they are than the teardrop forms they started out as. This is the stage when the water level needs to be lowered, to allow them to emerge onto land. This is when they begin to lose their gills and start to breathe atmospheric air.

The easiest method to do this is to transfer them and place the toad lot in an acrylic unit with a hood. Stand one end on a block of wood, and partially fill the enclosure. Give easy access to land via the gradual slope of the base of the terrarium, so the young toadlets can be able to come out of the water in time dictates. This land area must be covered with damp moss, helping to protect the fire belly toad lot from dehydration at this vulnerable stage, and keep the moss moist by regular spraying.

Once they have completed their metamorphosis, by about 12-14 weeks of age, the young toads will hunt for prey on land, with fruit flies being an ideal rearing food for them, although you will need to set up cultures in advance. They may continue to take bloodworm and daphnia, if this is accessible in a shallow container of water.

Growth and Diet

A varied diet is important. You might be able to collect some wild invertebrates too, if you have access to a garden, with aphids being a very valuable rearing food. If any of the toads do not appear to be thriving, it may be necessary to feed them in small containers, to ensure they are finding food without difficulty.

Hatchling (micro) crickets can also be provided, and should be sprinkled with a nutritional supplement. Do not neglect the lighting in the young toads' enclosure either, allowing them to synthesize their own Vitamin D, whilst helping to guarantee they develop a healthy skeletal structure.

Chapter Nine: Diseases and Health Requirements

Despite all your good care, your amphibian still could get sick or injured. First, you need to decide if your frog or toad is indeed sick or injured. If you have silently observed your web footed friend closely you probably are aware of its normal and usual behavior. Any unusual behavior may tip you off that something is wrong. It is instinctual for an animal in nature not to indicate illness since this is a sign of weakness which makes them vulnerable to predators and an easy target prey so, when they do display signs of illness, they may already be quite ill.

Understand, first of all, that a keeper shouldn't medicate an amphibian pet with human medications. This made for human medicine could be toxic to your frog or toad. Common sense and wise judgment calls are pretty vital as to whether you need professional medical help. If in doubt call your vet for advice. If you do bring your frog or toad to the vet, place it in a carrier. Or, in the case of a large amphibian, inside a pillowcase doubled with an untied plastic bag to prevent the mess a nervous amphibian is bound to make during the trip whilst inside your just-out-of-the-carwash, clean vehicle).

Carriers can be found and purchased at pet shops so be sure to invest in one as this will come in very handy for days like these. The carriers can also double up to be used as a safe holding place whilst you clean out their tank.

Be in the know and understand what you need to look out for if you suspect one of your fire belly toads to be ill. Understanding each of the fire belly toads under your care and getting used to certain behaviors that may suddenly change overnight, showing visible signs on their bodies or weird behavior they would otherwise not display are things you need to look out for a s a herp keeper with the best intentions for their wards.

Common Health Problems

Almost all pet frogs if healthy at the onset of joining your corner of the world tend to be pretty hardy and relatively long-lived. If your fire belly toad amphibian buddies have thus far fared well within a good span of many months and suddenly look sick, you will first need to evaluate their living conditions. Often enough, wrong temperatures, excessive levels of nitrites or ammonia in the water, fouled soil or substrate, and stress factors, such as excessive light exposure or overcrowding, could all contribute to illness and a depressed immune system. Righting these wrongs often causes frogs that display indications of sickness to become healthy once more.

If your amphibian buddy continues to appear or behave sick, strongly think about immediate veterinary care. It is unfortunate that with so few practitioners of the herp expertise, veterinary treatment can be quite costly with a basic exam costing many times over the cost of a single frog.

Factor in the costs of cultures and medications combined with the real possibility that sick frogs could die despite medical attention, and you might come to the conclusion that veterinary care is not a viable option. At any rate, the fire belly toads under your care do deserve humane treatment and must not be ignored and left to suffer without some sort of medical intervention nor must they be euthanized by inhumane methods.

To ensure the good health and long life of your pet amphibians, you must carefully design and maintain a terrarium so that the temperature, humidity levels, water quality, light, furnishings, topography, and diet given to them all meet the needs of your frogs

Checking the sound operation and accuracy of these conditions regularly will play a critical role in preventing the onset of disease in your amphibians. In addition, new animals have to be set apart and quarantined before being introduced to an enclosure with established pets.

Apart from flaws in husbandry, the introduction of sick animals is probably another common and definitely most significant reason of disease spread amongst established collections.

To recognize illness in frogs, toads look for the following signs:

Inactivity from a usual active frog or unusual out-of-nowhere behaviors

- o The initial sign to indicate malaise you may notice in your amphibian is abnormal behavior or a change of physical appearance.

- In fire-bellied toads, for example, inactivity and a horizontal stance instead of the normal front-raised posture are clear indications of illness.
- Terrestrial amphibians, which suddenly spend an excessive amount of time in the water is another indication of sickness.

Sudden or gradual weight loss

- Indications of weight loss in frogs are more pronounced in the abdominal area, which start to appear hollow.
- Eventually the outlines of the hip bones and backbones become prominent and skin may look saggy.

Body/abdominal bloating

- Bloating could be caused by extreme digestive gases
- Poor digestion due to respiratory infection
- Overeating
- Intestinal parasites
- Intestinal infection
- An oversized prey
- Gas bubble disease

Blotches on the skin

- o The frog might display angry red blotches (due to hemorrhaging)
- o White fuzzy blotches (due to fungi)

Eye cloudiness

- o When a frog's immune system is compromised and depressed, the stability of the eye lens is usually one of the first things to be affected by pathogens.
- o Unsuitable water quality which may be too acidic or too hard as well as high levels of toxins present in the water will also affect the lens of the frog.
- o Cloudy eyes are commonly secondary to other unseen problems. In rare cases, trauma to the head and orbit can directly result to an eye infection.

Edema is a general swelling of the frog's body, head, or limbs

- o A host of factors, from inadequate water quality to bacterial infections and kidney disease are some causes of edema.

Some symptoms that could indicate a problem exists:

Loss of Appetite

- This is a judgment call on your part since your frog or toad may slow down during winter months or it may be bored with same old fare. Switch up on a variety of foods before you determine if it is indeed sick. If you do conclude that it is ill, obtain a stool sample and get it to your frog doctor.
- If your frog is defecating bring the whole frog to the vet.

Listlessness

- When a formerly active frog or toad doesn't feel well and becomes listless. Almost all frogs and toads are not keen when it is disturbed and react by jumping away. Their actions will show you that they don't like the intrusion and disapprove of your show of affection.
- However if your frog or toad hardly reacts to your touch it is almost certain that it may be sick.
- If it appears to have difficulty moving, then take it as a sure sign of a problem.

Soaking much more than usual

- A frog or toad in utter dire straits seems to head for the water when they are not feeling in the pink. Whilst amphibians love to soak (and also how they drink) excessive bathing is not natural.

Injuries

- Obviously if your frog or toad is injured you will see that right away. They may have hurt themselves during their night time forays on a rough object in their habitat.

- Open wounds, deformed limbs etc. will be something you would certainly notice immediately whilst providing them exceptional daily room service.

- They make an effort to hide from us keepers and your frequent checking is most likely annoying for a frog that is trying to nap, but checking on them gives you peace of mind that your frog buddy is just A-OK and the he can live to nap another day.

Color

- o You know the normal color of your fire belly toad and if he is darker or paler than usual, things may not be right for your elusive pal.
- o Don't make a mistake and think otherwise but associate it with other symptoms.

Reddened belly and legs

- o This could be a symptom of the dreaded disease, aptly called, red leg
- o Gently press on the reddened area
- o If it stays red after you lift your finger, it could be red leg

Sores or blisters

- o This is definite indication of something not right with your buddy

Constantly yawning

- o A sure sign of spring disease
- o Frogs yawn when sleepy like we do, if you notice this, it could be this particular nasty disease with no known cure. Go to the vet.

No Poop to Scoop

- o No mess to clean up is obviously not normal
- o A frog or toads have to eliminate waste or it will become toxic.
- o It could have a blockage which is why it is a bad idea to put small rocks or pebbles in the tank since they can be ingested along with its food.
- o The frog or toad will probably also not be eating as well.
- o If you suspect this to be the cause and it turns out to be true, it will probably need surgery to correct the problem.

Bloating

- o Amphibians can "blow" up in an attempt to discourage enemies from preying on them and eventually deflate when the danger passes.
- o If your frog is frequently "blown" up, it may be retaining too much water (edema) and will need to see a frog doctor.

Cloudy eyes or blood in the eye

- o Blood in the eye is certainly a cause for concern.

- It may have injured himself, and often it is a sign of a generalized infection.
- Cloudy eyes could indicate too much fat in his diet and overfeeding. Domestically raised crickets can cause this.
- Feed crickets whole grains, veggies and fruit and not dog food.
- There is no cure for cloudy eyes so prevention is the best thing to do.

Chytrid

- The dreaded fungus affecting frogs.
- This disease is contagious and your frog may or may not show symptoms.
- Excessive shedding and "blushing" of the neck and belly and deep rosy mouth may be signs of Chytrid
- If you see these symptoms, have your frog seen by his vet so treatment can be started as soon as possible

Chapter 10: Summary and Quick Info

If there ever was an amphibian so easy to please in house and home, it would be the elusively friendly, skittishly amiable, gentle hopper with a guardedly toxic appeal; it would be our old buddy here, the fire belly toad.

It is our fervent wish that we have been able to lend a hand in getting you closer to deciding if the fire belly toad is in fact a suitable pet that would fit your lifestyle, complement your personality, brighten up your days, and be a fitting addition to your fold. Keep this book handy as a reference of sorts, or hand it over to someone equally interested in the care and husbandry of one of these colorfully adorable frogs.

To round up this book, check out a quick glance of pertinent, compiled information about this little guy with a big appetite and bigger personality. The next sections are a round up and a quick glance at some of the more important points about the *Bombina Orientalis* in a nugget of a nutshell.

Biological Information

- **Scientific Name:** Bombina Orientalis
- **Type:** Amphibian
- **Origin and Distribution:** China, Russia, Korea
- **Size in length:** 4cm - 7cm (1.5 – 3 inches)
- **Weight:** 20g - 80g (0.7oz - 2.8oz)
- **Top Speed:** 8km/h (5mph)
- **General Appearance:** has warty skin, green, red and black or yellow and black belly.
- **Growth Rate:** 2 years to adulthood Lifestyle: Solitary
- **Lifespan:** 10 to 15 years
- **Conservation Status:** Least Concern; not endangered
- **Color:** Black, Green, Grey, Brown, Yellow, Orange, Red

Fire Belly Toad as Pets

- **Behavioral characteristic:** enjoys solitude, does not mind the company as long as you leave it be and let it alone. A feisty fighter, a voracious eater
- **Defense Mechanism:** toxic appeal; it secretes toxic substance from its skin
- **Legal Requirement:** Not listed on the CITES endangered list

Purchasing and Selecting a Healthy Breed

- **Where to purchase a healthy breed:** Look for backyard breeders or buy directly from fire belly toad keepers with a successful breeding record.
- **Healthy Breed Characteristics:** full, plump body, alert, keen sense, no skin discoloration, mobile, great appetite
- **Characteristics of a Reputable Breeder:** An experienced herpetologist with recent breeding success

Requirements before Buying a Fire Belly Toad

- **Living in the Wild:** Mostly resides on swamps, marshes, river banks, slow moving water
- **Housing Size:** 20-gal terrarium

- **Where to Place:** on the floor
- **Accessories needed:** minimal; substrate, water dish, and aquatic plants
- **What to Avoid:** missing cleaning day; not changing water
- **Cleaning Frequency:** clean up every week; general cleaning each month
- **Maintenance:**
  - **Heating Temperature:** 70 – 82 Fahrenheit
  - **Humidity Temperature:** 30%
  - **Substrate Temperature:** equal to water temperature

Nutrition and Feeding

Diet: Carnivore
Favorite Food: Insects
Main Prey: Insects, Worms, Spiders
Predators: Foxes, Snakes, Birds

Handling Tips

- The skin of these frogs produces foul tasting toxins and could be harmful. Should you make the mistake of touching or rubbing your eyes after handling one of these little guys, you are sure to experience an intense burning sensation.

- You need to wash your hands and any part of your body the toad had come into contact with immediately.

Breeding and Requirements

Age of Maturity: Fire belly toad tadpoles a couple of years to come into full development and maturity

Breeding Season: around late spring

Clutch/Average Number of Eggs: 50-300 gooey, sticky eggs

Growth Rate/Length: An adult fire belly toad typically attains an adult length of about 2 ½ to 3 inches long.

Incubation Period: Tadpoles should come out from the egg jelly three to 10 days after being laid. It will take one to five months for the fire belly toad metamorphosis to be complete.

Nesting Requirements:

- The water temperature in the hatchling enclosure must be maintained at around 25°C (77°F)
- Separate the tadpoles as they grow into smaller groups of similar size
- Carry out partial water changes regularly;
- Check the water's quality

Diseases and Health Requirements

- Body/abdominal bloating
- Blotches on the skin
- Eye cloudiness
- Edema
- Chytrid

Glossary of Important Terms

Advertisement Call – mating call of frogs

Aggressive Call – territorial warning among male frogs; also "territorial call"

Amphibian – Vertebrates that spend part of their lives in water as well as on land. Other amphibians include salamanders and caecilians.

Amplexus – When a male positions himself on top of a female in order to fertilize her eggs

Anura – "tail-less"

Army – a group of frogs

Carnivore – meat-eater, including insectivores

Chorus – a large congregation of calling frogs

Chytridiomycosis – Also sometimes known as BD, a fungus that is deadly to most frogs

Cloaca – Opening in the rear end of a frog which allows for the passage of waste products, eggs, and sperm

Detritus – decayed plant and animal matter that collects at the bottom of a pond or water

Distress Call – call made to discourage predators

Ectothermic – external or environmental means of regulating body temperature

Frog – Any tailless amphibian of the order Anura

Froglet – a young frog that has just finished its metamorphosis from a tadpole

Herpetology – study of reptiles and amphibians

Insectivore – insect eater

Larva – Immature form or life-stage of amphibians

Metamorphosis – Profound change from one life stage to another, e.g., when tadpoles undergo a change and become frogs

Nictitating Membrane – a transparent inner eyelid

Pollywog – tadpoles

Frogspawn – collective term for frog eggs

Tadpole – larval stage of a frog's life cycle

Toe Pads – fleshy, disc-shaped sticky toes of tree frogs

Tympanum – The frog's eardrum

Vernal Pools – Temporary ponds formed with seasonal water such as snow melt or spring rains

Vocal Sac – skin pouches under a frog's chin that are inflated in order to make a call

Index

L

M

N

O

P

R

Photo Credits

Page 1 Photo by user Flickpicpete via Flickr.com, https://www.flickr.com/photos/flickpicpete/11868122953/

Page 4 Photo by user Flickpicpete via Flickr.com, https://www.flickr.com/photos/flickpicpete/6892698567/

Page 15 Photo by user Flickpicpete via Flickr.com, https://www.flickr.com/photos/flickpicpete/15015600539/

Page 24 Photo by user Robert Verzo via Flickr.com, https://www.flickr.com/photos/verzo/6314560936/

Page 42 Photo by user Alexandre Roux via Flickr.com, https://www.flickr.com/photos/30142279@N07/32744242453/

Page 58 Photo by user Robert Verzo via Flickr.com, https://www.flickr.com/photos/verzo/3285583512/

Page 71 Photo by user David Nunn via Flickr.com, https://www.flickr.com/photos/davidnunn/13226920635/

Page 75 Photo by user Josh More via Flickr.com,
https://www.flickr.com/photos/guppiecat/8631021565/

Page 87 Photo by user Laurent Lebols via Flickr.com,
https://www.flickr.com/photos/cheloran/5837326614/

Page 91 Photo by user Charles Kaiser via Flickr.com,
https://www.flickr.com/photos/ckaiserca/452846698/

Page 103 Photo by user Dagget2 via Flickr.com,
https://www.flickr.com/photos/dagget2/7848709864/

References

"Fire – Bellied Toad" Wikipedia.org
https://en.wikipedia.org/wiki/Fire-bellied_toad#Species

"Oriental Fire-Bellied Toad" National Geographic
http://www.nationalgeographic.com/animals/amphibians/o/
oriental-fire-bellied-toad/

"Fire – Bellied Toad Facts" Softschools.com
http://www.softschools.com/facts/animals/firebellied_toad_f
acts/296/

"Fire Belly Toads" LLLReptile.com
https://www.lllreptile.com/articles/144-fire-belly-toads/

"The Oriental fire-bellied Toad" PetInfoClub.com
https://www.petinfoclub.com/Exotics/Profiles/FrogsToads/O
riental_fire-bellied_toad.aspx

"Citing The IUCN Red List" IUCNRedlist.org
http://www.iucnredlist.org/about/citing

"Sick Frogs And Salamanders" Reptiles Magazine
http://www.reptilesmagazine.com/Frogs-Amphibians/Sick-
Frogs-And-Amphibians/

"Bombina orientalis" Amphibiaweb.org
http://amphibiaweb.org/cgi/amphib_query?where-
genus=Bombina&where-species=orientalis

**"The Differences between Girl and Boy Fire-Bellied
Toads"** Mom.me
http://animals.mom.me/differences-between-girl-boy-
firebellied-toads-6490.html

"Toadily Toads Most Frequently Asked Questions"
ToadilyToads.com
http://www.toadilytoads.com/toadilytoads_faqs.html#Anch
or-35882

"The Frog Doctor" Frogdaze.com
http://www.frogdaze.com/the-frog-doctor.html

"Feed Your Fire-Bellied Toads the Right Foods"
Reptiles Magazine
http://www.reptilesmagazine.com/Frogs-
Amphibians/Feeding-Fire-Bellied-Toads/

"How to Care for Fire Belly Toads" Wikihow.com
http://www.wikihow.com/Care-for-Fire-Belly-Toads

Feeding Baby
Cynthia Cherry
978-1941070000

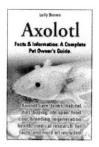

Axolotl
Lolly Brown
978-0989658430

Dysautonomia, POTS
Syndrome
Frederick Earlstein
978-0989658485

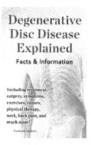

Degenerative Disc
Disease Explained
Frederick Earlstein
978-0989658485

Sinusitis, Hay Fever,
Allergic Rhinitis Explained
Frederick Earlstein
978-1941070024

Wicca
Riley Star
978-1941070130

Zombie Apocalypse
Rex Cutty
978-1941070154

Capybara
Lolly Brown
978-1941070062

Eels As Pets
Lolly Brown
978-1941070167

Scabies and Lice Explained
Frederick Earlstein
978-1941070017

Saltwater Fish As Pets
Lolly Brown
978-0989658461

Torticollis Explained
Frederick Earlstein
978-1941070055

Kennel Cough
Lolly Brown
978-0989658409

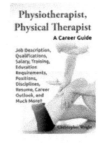

Physiotherapist, Physical
Therapist
Christopher Wright
978-0989658492

Rats, Mice, and Dormice
As Pets
Lolly Brown
978-1941070079

Wallaby and Wallaroo Care
Lolly Brown
978-1941070031

Bodybuilding Supplements
Explained
Jon Shelton
978-1941070239

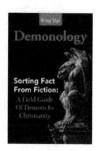

Demonology
Riley Star
978-19401070314

Pigeon Racing
Lolly Brown
978-1941070307

Dwarf Hamster
Lolly Brown
978-1941070390

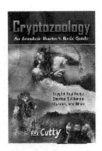

Cryptozoology
Rex Cutty
978-1941070406

Eye Strain
Frederick Earlstein
978-1941070369

Inez The Miniature Elephant
Asher Ray
978-1941070353

Vampire Apocalypse
Rex Cutty
978-1941070321